Chances are
We'll go down in history.
When they want to see
How true love should be
They'll just look at us.

Look At Us, by Vince Gill & Max Barnes

LOOK AT US

A Love Story

(What Life, Love, & Loss Taught Me About Romance)

by

Kenneth N. Myers

Mayeux Press
DENISON, TEXAS

Look At Us

Myers, Kenneth Neal, 1959-
Look At Us/Kenneth N. Myers

Cover design: Michael Peterson
Cover photography: Annie Wymore

Published by Mayeux Press
561 Bailey Drive, Denison TX 75021

In Loving Memory
of
Shirley Mae

Table of Contents

Foreword

Shirley Mae McSorley Myers passed away unexpectedly at the age of 58 on January 9, 2017, after nearly forty years of being my wonderful wife. During her short illness, and after we lost her, I received notes from many people commenting on the love we had for one another. I'm sharing these now, not because of anything special on my part, but because Shirley was so easy to love, she made me look good doing it:

Your love for her is beautiful.

Your love for your wife mirrors the love that Christ has for the Church. As it should.

I would love to be loved like that.

You were a blessed man in having her as a wife and friend and I know your heart is breaking...but take stock in the fact that you had the love story to end all stories...you had the real Princess Bride fairy tale love story that only a fraction of a fraction are blessed to experience.

I've always admired your marriage. From your wedding day (which is the first wedding I remember attending) to these wonderful words of advice...what a great example you and Shirley have been.

Your romance is lighting up my life right now. I wish I had been in the audience from the beginning. There are not many like yours in the world. Hang tight, ever so tight to the light of God that held you together.

Not long after this, I received several notes from people suggesting I write a book about the love Shirley and I shared - not so much as a personal biography, but as a book of hints for other couples. One young husband told me that the love between Shirley and me served as a model for him and his newlywed wife. A wife wrote me and jokingly said that I needed to write a book on romance so her husband could read it!

In the mid 1800s, Charles Spurgeon wrote a six volume commentary on Psalms titled *The Treasury of David*. The original version contained a section called *Hints To The Village Preacher.* This "Prince of Preachers", who was preaching to a congregation of 6,000 by the time he was 19, listed ideas that other preachers might use as a springboard for their own sermons.

By no means do I consider myself a "prince of husbands," quite the opposite actually, however I believe I have some insights to share with other men - especially young husbands - which can enrich their relationships with their wives, and perhaps even save them some from some unnecessary bumps along the way. I hope and pray that this book and the love that Shirley and I shared will help other couples not only grow in their love, but also find ways to celebrate that love in their lives.

Phoenix, AZ, August 31, 2017

Chapter One

How I Found The Love Of My Life

I knew she was mine the moment I saw her. Never mind that I was only 17 and had never dated a girl before in my entire life; I knew this was the woman I was going to marry.

When I was young, I was incredibly awkward and shy around the girls, especially if I was attracted to them. Sure, I had female friends at school and at church, but I was clueless about how to handle myself around a girl I "liked." At the risk of dredging up feelings of embarrassment and humiliation, I'll share just two of my more awkward experiences.

Wallflower

Tenth grade. Journalism class. No desks, just big tables we all sat around. Mrs. Casey was my all time favorite school teacher, and while she taught the material well, she was also fun and relaxed and was pretty easygoing during our free time. The year was 1975 and flavored lip gloss had just hit the market and was all the rage. I found myself sitting at a table with probably half a dozen girls and one of them pulled out a tube of strawberry lip gloss and all the girls were talking about it. I asked, "Does it really taste like strawberries?" That's when Debbie, the cutest girl in class, rolled the tube across her lips and said, "Kiss me and find out!"

I'm quite sure my face turned a hundred shades of red; I had never kissed a girl.

That's when I did the most stupid thing a teenage boy could do. With my heart pounding in my chest, I leaned forward toward beautiful Debbie's lips…and gave her my cheek to kiss! Debbie laughed and said, "Silly - how can you taste it if I kiss your cheek?" Every girl at the table laughed and I sank into humiliating embarrassment. In just a few seconds that seemed like hours, I missed the chance for my first kiss to be from the prettiest and sweetest girl in class, and publicly made a fool of myself. Sigh.

There was another girl that I had a crush on that lasted several years, but I never found the inner strength to follow up on my feelings. Cynthia was a beautiful Italian girl who was popular and sweet and way out of my league in my mind.

One day a good friend of mine said, "Let's ride our bikes over to her house and visit." So, on a hot summer afternoon we pedaled a couple of miles across town toward her house. When we arrived, my heart was once again pounding in my chest as my friend Ricky knocked on her front door. She answered the knock, came out and sat on the front porch with us, and visited for about 20 minutes. Of course, Ricky did every bit of the talking and I sat there like a dumb kid (dumb in both senses of the word: ignorant and completely unable to utter a single word). The whole bike ride back home my buddy Ricky cajoled me about my ridiculous bump on a log performance. Another missed opportunity!

There was something deep in my teenage psyche that made me freeze up in the presence of a girl I found attractive. These are only two of the many stories I could tell, but I will spare you of further cringing and pity and leave the rest unwritten.

The Missionary's Daughter I Didn't Want To Meet

When I was 17 our church youth group was led by a woman named Anita who was about 10 years older than I and was the daughter of a missionary in Mexico who our church supported. She talked now and again about her little sister and how I should meet her someday. I had absolutely zero interest in meeting Anita's sister who lived 550 miles away from me in the border town of Zapata, Texas.

In the early summer of 1976 I went with a couple of friends to a "Jesus Festival" in Topeka, Kansas where, for three days, Larry Norman, Jamie Owens, Darrell Mansfield, and about 40 others artists performed day and night on half a dozen different stages scattered throughout a park. When Anita learned about the concert she said I should invite her little sister. Nope. Not excited about the prospect. I didn't know this girl, had never met her, and wasn't interested in the least.

At the time my dad had a little Cessna plane and he flew my friends and me up to the concert. While we were enjoying the Christian rock music echoing through the park, Dad flew back to Denison to lead the church services that weekend. His guest speaker that weekend was Anita's father, missionary Jerry McSorley. And this missionary had with him on the trip Anita's little sister, the girl I didn't care to meet. Imagine my embarrassment when I returned and discovered that my father had publicly, from the pulpit, remarked that he wished his son had been in town to meet this missionary's daughter!

Later in the summer, I got a phone call from Anita asking if she could borrow a record of mine. "Can I borrow your Barry McGuire *Seeds* album? Can you drive it over to my house?" I hopped into my brown 1970 Cougar and headed to Sherman to drop off the album. I pulled into Anita's driveway, parked the car, and walked to the front door to deliver the music of Mr. McGuire.

Knock. Knock-knock. A few seconds later the door opened and this spectacularly beautiful 18-year-old angel dressed in peach shorts and a matching top welcomed me in. It was Anita's sister! My juvenile heart leapt into my throat and from out of nowhere I said to myself, "I'm going to marry this woman!"

Shirley Mae McSorley ushered me into the house where Anita, Anita's husband Don, and her mother and father - Betty and Jerry McSorley - sat visiting in the living room. Introductions were made, the album was delivered, and every bit of my shyness and awkwardness disappeared into thin air.

I actually talked to Shirley! This was a milestone for me, though I didn't realize it at the moment. Here I was talking and laughing with a real life beautiful young woman with whom I was completely smitten. I have no idea how long I stayed at Anita's home that night, but it was several hours. Shirley and I talked the whole time, and we laughed and joked and I completely forgot anyone else was in the room. When I did finally bid farewell to everyone, Shirley escorted me to the door and I am pretty sure that I floated back to my car and drove away.

My First And Only Girlfriend

It turns out that Shirley had come to
Sherman to explore the possibility of
moving in with her sister and attending
Grayson County College. She was about to
venture forward into her next phase of
education, and I was about to have my life
turned upside down.

For a couple of years my two best
friends, Randy Thacker and David Neal,
had been making plans with me for our
future. We were going to graduate from
high school. We were going to take a year
off before college and hike the Appalachian
Trail together. We had fantasies of buying
an old three-story house in Denison and
turning it into a stellar bachelors pad.
Shirley threw all these plans and fantasies
into complete disarray! I was smitten. I
was lovesick. Nothing else mattered but
having Shirley in my life.

After Shirley moved to Sherman, I was
with her every chance I got. I remember

going to church not long after we had met and clambering past a row of girls in order to squeeze myself into the pew next to Shirley. One of the girls who liked me warned Shirley not to get her hopes up and cautioned her that I was fickle and wouldn't keep an interest in her for very long. Of course, it had nothing to do with being fickle and everything to do with being shell-shocked around the ladies.

Our first "date" came in the autumn of 1976. I was the editor-in-chief of the school newspaper my senior year, and I had been assigned by Mrs. Casey to write an article on "the glowing tombstone" in Pottsboro, about half a dozen miles west of Denison. I picked Shirley up in my Cougar, stopped at a drive-in restaurant and got her a diet Dr Pepper, and headed west. Yes, our very first date was going to a cemetery! Talk about romance. I must admit, in retrospect, that this was a pretty good idea. In a little country cemetery, far away from any streetlights, there was one tombstone in the middle of the grounds that seemed to glow at night. It was eerie; downright spooky.

We drove to Pottsboro and found the cemetery and I unpacked my camera to get a shot of the mysterious stone. The Plymouth Cougar had bucket seats, but Shirley leaned a little closer to me on the way back home, perhaps from a touch of fright, or perhaps from a touch of love. Maybe a little of both. It wasn't long after that night that Shirley loved being close to me so much that her "seat" in the car became that little hump between the bucket seats. This was the 1970s before there were seatbelt laws and Shirley always chose to climb up and ride on the uncomfortable console just so she could be close to me.

Being the romantic klutz that I was, our first kiss didn't come for probably a month or two after that magical meeting over the Barry McGuire album. I didn't even hold hands with her for the first half-dozen times we went out. One day, as we Anita's through the backyard gate, our hands brushed, then clasped, almost accidentally. I was innocent, and this was heaven to me.

But I couldn't muster up the nerve to kiss her!

Whereas I had never dated a girl before Shirley, she was well-schooled in that department. Shirley was incredibly popular in school, and popular with the boys. She had had a string of boyfriends, both in Zapata and in other places where she had traveled with her family as her father itinerated to raise support for the missions in Mexico. A boyfriend for a while from a church in Wisconsin. Another for a while from a church camp in Michigan. A few different fellows from school in Zapata. A young missionary named Steve Hodges who worked in Mexico with her father; his family had been close to the McSorleys for decades, and Shirley was even named after his mother.

That first kiss, which I simply couldn't muster up the courage to give, was taken care of at Shirley's initiative. Just a light, momentarily lingering kiss on the lips, but I'm pretty sure it was the best thing that had ever happened to me in my life up to that point.

Getting Hitched

We started dating in October of 1976 and were married nine months later, at Evangel Temple Assemblies of God Church in Denison, on July 30, 1977, on my father's 40th birthday. I am in no way suggesting that our courtship was all roses and wine (in fact, drinking wine was considered a sin in our circles in those days, but our courtship wasn't even all roses). We fought a lot, sometimes like cats and dogs. The night before the wedding, after friends and family were already in town, we had a knock-down-drag-out fight that almost ended the whole thing. As we sat on the porch steps of the house we were moving into, Shirley said to me, "It's not too late to change your mind." But even in the midst of the worst arguments we deeply loved one another. I had found the love of my life, and she had found hers.

Not that I didn't face some tough competition. When I drove to Zapata to meet the rest of her family, one of her old boyfriends came to see her to try to talk her out of choosing me. I was too inexperienced in the ways of love to even do anything about it, and I sat in her parents' living room while her old boyfriend sat out on the porch with her giving it his one last shot. And a week or two before we got married, her lifelong friend and sometime-romance, Steve Hodges, hopped on a motorcycle and drove 1,500 miles all the way from Acapulco, Mexico to Sherman, Texas to try to win her back. I didn't know about his intentions until after the fact, but sitting at the kitchen table in Anita's house one morning Shirley asked Steve what he wanted for breakfast, and he said, "To marry you."

Thankfully, this beautiful, godly, popular, sexy young woman chose me over all other suitors, and we were married eight weeks after I graduated from high school. So much for the Appalachian Trail and the cool three-story bachelors pad. Randy joined the Marines, David joined the Navy, and I joined Shirley in wedded bliss.

Chapter Two

How I Lost
The Love Of My Life

We were going to grow old together. We dreamed and talked about what it would be like to be together in our 80s. For our 40th anniversary we were going to do something big - maybe a trip to the Caribbean, maybe a couple of weeks in Ireland.

All of that began to change on Christmas night, 2016. My daughter Stormie was at home with us, and my son

Ken and his boys, Ken and Elijah, were
visiting for the holiday. It was a low-key
celebration and we were all just hanging
out at the house enjoying one another's
company. The day before, Shirley thought
she was coming down with a cold or maybe
an allergy attack and went to bed early
after we had exchanged gifts. After a
supper of leftovers from Christmas dinner
Shirley again retired early, not feeling well.

Christmas With Pneumonia

Shirley woke me up around 3:00 in the
morning and said she couldn't breathe. I
asked if she thought she needed to go to
the emergency room and she rasped out
that she did. I hurriedly told the kids what
was going on, loaded her into the car, and
drove as fast as I could to Texoma Medical
Center where she was whisked into a room
and in less than a minute had all kinds of
medical people hooking her up to oxygen
and monitors and taking vitals. After a
couple of hours a doctor walked in and
announced, "Congratulations! You have

double pneumonia!" He gave her some instructions and some medicine and released us to go back home with orders for bedrest and a caution to come back if things got worse.

Shirley spent a restless night and slept late the next morning, staying in bed most of the day after Christmas, getting up only for short periods to visit with the kids. At about 2:00 the next morning, Tuesday the 27th, she woke me again. "I think I need to go back to the hospital." She was having great difficulty breathing and was scared.

I loaded her up again and drove as fast as I could back to the ER where she was admitted to the hospital. Dad and Mom had left for a trip to Florida where he was scheduled to speak in churches, and I called and let them know what was going on. He offered to turn around and head home, but I insisted they keep their schedule and promised to keep them posted.

Once she was admitted and again hooked up to oxygen and IVs and all kinds of monitors, the doctors discovered that Shirley not only had double pneumonia, but also some kind of infection in her bloodstream; sepsis perhaps. Things spiraled from there. She simply wasn't getting enough oxygen with the normal mask, so they brought in a full-faced pressurized mask that forced oxygen into the lungs. It made her miserable and she vacillated between trying to cooperate with the mask and trying to rip it off. No matter what they tried, she wasn't getting the oxygen she needed. On Thursday the doctors decided to move her to ICU and put her in an induced coma and on a ventilator, hoping to give her body some rest and allow oxygen to get back into her system. The medical team still couldn't figure out what was causing the infection, so they had her on three different antibiotics trying to fight it. It tore me apart to see my poor, sweet wife lying there unconscious and hooked up to all kinds of machines. How could this be? Just a few days ago she was healthy and happy and enjoying time with her family.

I put out a post to all my Facebook friends, asking them to pray for Shirley:

My honey is worse than we knew. Severe double pneumonia. It showed up a lot worse on CT than on x-ray. And sepsis. They are intubating her for at least 48 hours. Y'all pray. My heart is breaking for her.

Rollercoaster

By 5 p.m. things were improving. A nurse came to debrief me and said that Shirley had been very hard to sedate and that they had given her "a gargantuan amount of sedatives" before she finally gave in to rest. Her white blood cell count was normal and it appeared the infection had been knocked out by all the antibiotics. Hopefully, she said, Shirley could be extubated within the next 36 hours. Family members and friends were in the waiting room, and everyone's hopes elevated at the news. Shirley was getting better!

And then she got worse. This was turning into a rollercoaster ride both for Shirley's physical condition and everyone else's emotions. By Thursday afternoon the infection had returned. The doctors decided to do a bronchoscope to look around in her lungs and attempt to remove anything in them that might be causing difficulties. I kept posting updates on Facebook and other social media and by now there were literally hundreds of people around the world praying for her recovery and offering me words of comfort and support. One woman wrote, "She's always been my idea of the Proverbs 31 woman. You are blessed to have her and she is blessed to have you. She must be so uncomfortable. Praying hard for God's healing touch on every part of her body!"

Then things got better again. By now days and nights had merged into a blur of time as family and friends waited and prayed for Shirley's recovery. At noon on Friday the 30th, I posted another update to Facebook:

So, they are weaning her off the stronger sedative now in hopes that they can get her awake sometime late this afternoon - 4 or 5 is the most optimistic. Her white cell count is normal, which is great. If they can wake her up without panic, they want to keep the tube in for half an hour or so, and have her breathe on her own, and see if she can keep the oxygen level up. If she can, they'll remove the tube. They are still waiting (up to 48 more hours) for all the test results to come back. The BEST CASE scenario is she goes home Tuesday or Wednesday, and takes another week to ten days to recover there. PLEASE PRAY that she wake up OK and not panic with that tube stuck down her throat.

By late afternoon on Friday the doctors had weaned Shirley off the sedatives with the hope of her breathing on her own and being able to take the tube out of her throat. When she became somewhat alert they turned the breathing machine off and the nurse encouraged her to breathe on her own. But after about 10 minutes, she was breathing so hard and short (50 breaths a minute and not oxygenating) that they had to put her back under, back on the machine, and promised to try again the next day. The nurse told me that about 60 to 70 percent of patients fail to come off the breathing machine on the first attempt. He cautioned all of us that we shouldn't go into "panic mode." This was actually the typical response for a patient, and tomorrow or the next day, hopefully, she would come off the machine more easily.

Early in the evening on Saturday, the doctors tried once again to take Shirley off the sedation. She did better than the day before, but she was still not cooperative enough to take her off the ventilator. I updated her friends and family on Facebook:

They're keeping her partially sedated and trying again in the morning. She's been conscious enough to look me in the eyes and to squeeze my hand, and she's obviously confused about what's going on. I hurt so much for her. They told me to not even talk to her because the less stimulation the better right now so she can rest. Sigh.

New Year's Day

Sunday, January 1, 2017. A new day. A new year. A week now since this whole thing started on Christmas night. And finally, some good news.

At 7:15 a.m. the doctors and nurses came in and roused Shirley. When they woke her up she was more responsive and cognizant than she had been during the previous two attempts, and I was praying she would cooperate with them and would have the strength of will and of lung power to pass the test they had planned for her later in the morning. If she passed the breathing test, the nurse told me, they would extract the tube from her throat and lungs and get her back on a normal oxygen mask.

Since Shirley had been in the hospital I had been keeping up with world news via the internet. On New Year's Eve William Christopher, the actor who played Father Mulcahey on *M*A*S*H*, passed away at the age of 84. A few days before that, on

December 27, the actress Carrie Fisher died, followed the very next day by her mother, Debbie Reynolds. Death was in the news, but thankfully it appeared that Shirley was on the mend.

At noon the tube was finally removed from Shirley's throat. The nurse asked her a series of questions to ascertain her mental state.

> Nurse: "Do you know his name?"
> Shirley: "Ken."
> Nurse: "Do you know your name?"
> Shirley: "Shirley Myers."
> Nurse: "Do you know what year it is?"
> Shirley: "2016."
> Nurse: "Wrong, it's 2017!"

Shirley had a befuddled look on her face. She had been "out of it" and in very rough shape for four days, and here she was waking up in a whole new year.

When she came out of sedation but still couldn't easily speak, Shirley asked for a writing board and scribbled some illegible marks for me to read. She was disgruntled that I couldn't make out what she was trying to write - it looked like three words, but made no sense whatsoever. Later she told me she had written, "You weren't there."

When she came out of sedation she was "tripping," and was very antagonistic toward me. She didn't want me to touch her. Every time I reached out to gently touch her arm she pulled away and vigorously shook her head and muttered, "NO!" When I said, "I love you," she mouthed back, "Shut. Up." In her mind, she told me after she was alert, it wasn't me who was there beside her. "You weren't there." It was some evil creature trying to disguise itself as me, and if it touched her she would die, along with all her family.

My poor baby. I felt so sorry for her. After she told me her nightmarish tale, she reached her hand out and touched my arm and, looking me deeply in the eyes with those gorgeous brown eyes I had fallen in love with 40 years before, said very intently, "I adore you." She had experienced so much agony, both physically and mentally. But now I had her back and things were looking up.

The Road Toward Recovery...And Home

By Tuesday morning, the nurses had removed the feeding tube and although she was incredibly weak and could hardly speak, Shirley was back to being her old self and was clearly improving. Everyone who had been praying for her and keeping up with the situation breathed a sigh of relief and gave thanks to God. One dear friend spoke what everyone was feeling: "Please let her know how proud we all are of her fight towards recovery. And encourage her to take it slow from here to avoid setbacks. Feeling relieved!"

Tuesday was a day of progress. Shirley posted on Facebook, "I'm back. And I love you all! I'm still in the hospital, but I'm getting stronger." She had a few visitors, walked with assistance to the bathroom, and sat up for the nurses to shampoo her hair. After walking a few steps, she needed oxygen to regain her strength, and she went to sleep a little shaky and short-breathed. All day Wednesday was a no-visitor day so she could spend it recuperating.

By Thursday Shirley had made remarkable improvement and was off all the tubes and wires and monitors except the heart monitor. The doctors came in and announced that she could go home on Friday. Everyone was thrilled. Shirley was so very tired of being in that hospital, being sick, and being out of the loop with the rest of the world. She was practically silly with the anticipation of finally getting better and going home. For the next several weeks or even months she would be on bedrest, with a physical therapist visiting frequently, but she would be home, the place she loved more than anywhere else in the world.

I left her side late Thursday morning and went to Walmart and Target to buy all kinds of things to welcome her home. I bought new sheets for the bed; two new pairs of pajamas; a new robe; a new shoe rack to organize all her shoes in the closet; an armload of cleaning supplies. After the shopping spree I went home and worked hard cleaning our bedroom and bathroom, putting on the new sheets, cleaning up the closet and arranging her shoes. I was going to treat her like a queen and pamper her for the next two weeks, and she was going to be so happy to see her home all fresh and clean and cozy.

I checked in on Shirley in the late afternoon and she told me she was starving for enchiladas, and would I please bring her some. So I cleaned myself up, got two orders of enchiladas to go, and went back up to the hospital. Shirley had been up walking the halls, without oxygen, and breathing well on her own. She was tired now, but devoured her favorite meal while we watched a TV show together.

I bet we said the words, "I love you," 20 times as we sat together, and after the show was over she told me that she was tired and was going to try to sleep. I told her I was going home to finish making things ready for her homecoming and that I would see her in the morning. I kissed her goodnight, we both said, "I love you," one more time, and I headed for the house. Little did I know that this was the last time I would hear her say those cherished words.

On the way home I got a text from my baby. Just a written reminder of what I'd heard so many times that evening:

"I love you."

About an hour later, while I was on my hands and knees scrubbing the bathroom floor, my phone rang. "Mr. Myers, I am calling from TMC. You need to come immediately. Your wife has gone into cardiac arrest."

Losing The Love Of My Life

By the time I got to the hospital Shirley had been moved back to ICU, intubated, and sedated. The doctor came to speak with me and apprise me of the situation as he best understood it. Shirley had indeed gone to sleep after I left her. Tiffany, a patient care tech with whom Shirley had bonded and become friends, was the last person to speak to her when she made her evening rounds checking on her. They had joked and laughed and Shirley had told her, like she had me, that she was going to try to get some sleep. Sometime between Tiffany leaving and about 10:30, Shirley simply stopped breathing. Maybe she fell into a good, deep sleep and her weak lungs just tired out. But she went without oxygen for several minutes before her heart stopped and set off the alarms.

When they were alerted by the heart monitor, a team of aids, nurses, and doctors rushed in to try and revive her. They performed CPR and broke several of her ribs in the process. The team ended up having to use the shock cart and by the time they revived her they had been working on her for fifteen minutes, and this didn't include however long she had been without oxygen between the time she stopped breathing and the time her heart stopped and tripped the alarm. When her heart stopped, Shirley aspirated, so even when she did revive her lungs were filled with material she had sucked in during the aspiration. It didn't look good.

I called my parents in Florida and they immediately began the long drive back home. I called our sons, and Shirley's family, and everyone began making the journey toward Sherman. What the hell had happened? Shirley was *better*. She was coming home, for heaven's sake! How could this be real?

This was all such a shock. In an instant things had changed. What had been the joyous hope that all this was finally over turned into the realization that we may be in for a very long ordeal, or even death. On Friday morning, the morning I was supposed to be bringing my dear wife back home and treating her like royalty, the doctors informed me that they were putting her into hyperthermia, cooling her body down for the next 24 to 48 hours, because she was exhibiting severe shaking at any stimulus (called startle response), and this was an indication of some brain damage, but they wouldn't know for a day or two how severe it was. The best-case scenario, I was told, was that the damage might be minor and she could re-pattern her brain. The worst case scenario was that we would have to make a decision about keeping her alive.

Saturday was a day of waiting and there was nothing anyone could do but pray. By Sunday morning family had arrived and the waiting room was filled with probably 50 friends and family members. A steady stream of local pastors passed through, each one coming to offer prayers and love.

Just before noon on Sunday we were informed that the damage to Shirley's brain was severe, and that the kids and I needed to talk together and make a decision. If we tried to save her, we were told, she would be on life support for a minimum of several months before they could even attempt for her to breathe on her own, and even if she could, she would be severely mentally impaired, not knowing who she was or who any of us were.

Shirley's entire family and I spent the rest of the day in anguish. Some couldn't believe this was happening and were thinking they had heard God promise a miracle of recovery. Others were facing the reality of the inevitable. Everyone was shocked and heartbroken.

On the morning of Monday, January 9, exactly two weeks after this unimaginable episode began, Stormie, Ken, Jay, and I met with a team of doctors and gave them instructions to take Shirley off life support. The night before, I had posted on Facebook, "I am losing the light of my life," and a friend responded, "Your romance is lighting up my life right now. I wish I had been in the audience from the beginning.

There are not many like your's in the world. Hang tight, ever so tight to the light of God that held you together."

It hit me hard, about this time, that my love for Shirley had a selfish streak to it. I loved her deeply for herself, but I also loved her so much because of what she meant *to me*. As I pondered this, the words to *As The Ruins Fall*, a poem by C.S. Lewis that is the only poem I have ever memorized came flooding back to my mind:

> *All this is flashy rhetoric about loving you.*
> *I never had a selfless thought since I was born.*
> *I am mercenary and self-seeking through and through:*
> *I want God, you, all friends, merely to serve my turn.*
> *Peace, re-assurance, pleasure, are the goals I seek,*
> *I cannot crawl one inch outside my proper skin:*
> *I talk of love - a scholar's parrot may talk Greek -*

*But, self-imprisoned, always ends where I
begin.
Only that now you have taught me (but
how late) my lack.
I see the chasm.
And everything you are was making
My heart into a bridge by which I might
get back
From exile, and grow man.
And now the bridge is breaking.
For this I bless you as the ruin falls.
The pains You give me are more precious
than all other gains.*

Saying Goodbye For The Last Time

It took several hours before the medical team could take Shirley off life support, and the nurse in charge told us there was really no way of knowing how long it would take for her to pass away. It could happen in a moment, or it could take a day. Her educated guess was that it would be a few hours, because, "she has a strong heart." After all the tubes and wires and masks were removed, Shirley's sisters and brother, our children, and I gathered in the room, sometimes as the whole group, sometimes just one or two, speaking and singing to her and each of us telling her goodbye. At one point, I escorted my grandsons, Ken and Elijah, back to the little room where Shirley was, and gave them each some personal time with Grandma.

As the day wore on, all the family gathered around her. We prayed the "Our Father." We sang *It Is Well With My Soul:*

> *When peace like a river attendeth my way,*
> *When sorrows like sea billows roll,*
> *Whatever my lot, thou hast taught me to say,*
> *It is well, it is well with my should.*

I sang over her the version of *O Gracious Light* (the oldest known hymn in Christianity) that she had written music for:

> *...Now as we come to the setting of the sun*
> *and our eyes behold the vesper light,*
> *we sing your praises O God, Father, Son, and*
> *Holy Spirit,*

We sing your praises O God, Father, Son, and
Holy Spirit,
You are worthy at all times to be praised by
happy voices,
O Son of God, O giver of life,
And to be glorified through all the world.

And I leaned over her and softly sang,

Lay down my dear sister, lay down and take
your rest.
I want to lay your head upon your Savior's
breast.
I love you, but Jesus loves you best.
I bid you goodnight, goodnight, goodnight.

And then, like that, she was gone. 7:55
p.m., January 9, 2017.

I knew it was coming. We all knew it
was coming. But when she breathed her
last little breath and the color left her face,
all I could think to myself was, No! This
isn't supposed to happen! This can't
happen! She isn't supposed to die!

My wife, the love of my life, my best
friend and lover and partner in crime and

confidant and half of my soul, slipped from this world into the next. It was the most grievous thing I have ever experienced. The Bible says that we believers, "do not grieve as others do who have no hope." But, my God, we do still grieve.

With all her siblings and children present, I celebrated last rites and the Ministration at the Time of Death from the prayerbook, with all her family joining in, praying that God receive Shirley's soul into the arms of his love. After everyone else had left the room I asked the nurse for some privacy, and I laid beside my beautiful bride and cried and told her goodbye for the final time. I walked backward out of the room and down the hallway, keeping my gaze on her until I could see her no more.

Chapter Three

Learning The Hard Way

The last time I sang to Shirley was at her bedside as she was slipping out of this world. The first time I sang to her was on July 30, 1977 as we exchanged vows before a small gathering of friends and family. We were so poor when we got married! I mean, not poor in the sense of destitute, but young, and simple, and not having much money at all. I was the son of a pastor and she was the daughter of a missionary and neither of our families were flush with money. I was two months out of high school and working as a barber and she was a secretary at Olsen Bodies in Sherman. I think between the two of us we probably made about $350 a week, so our wedding was not the elaborate staging that so many are today.

Follow Me

Come wedding time we scraped together just enough to get by. Shirley's sister Anita made her simple wedding dress, a cute little white sundress that came to just below her knees. Our rehearsal dinner was, if I remember correctly, the joint effort of ladies from church bringing crock pots and trays of food for everyone in attendance. Our wedding rings cost a total of $148 and were not much more than scrap metal. But we sang to each other.

Shirley and I were both John Denver fans and we chose two of his songs to sing to one another in the ceremony. I chose *Follow Me:*

*Follow me, where I go, what I do and who I
know,
Make it part of you to be a part of me.
Follow me up and down, all the way and all
around,
Take my hand and say you'll follow me.*

And she sang *For Baby:*

*I'll walk in the rain by your side,
I'll cling to the warmth of your hand,
I'll do anything to keep you satisfied,
I'll love you more than anybody can.
And the wind will whisper your name to me,
Little birds will sing along in time,
Leaves will bow down, when you walk by,
And morning bells will chime.*

In retrospect those songs are quite
innocent, and perhaps a little cheesy, but
they sure captured our devotion to one
another. And here is the important thing:
Shirley did follow me. For better or for
worse. Even when I was young and stupid
(not to mention when I was an old man
and stupid). She followed me when any
person in their right mind wouldn't have.
She followed me when I was too
inexperienced to be leading. She followed

53

me 1,500 miles from her hometown to pastor a church in northern Wisconsin. She followed me from our Pentecostal tradition into the Anglican faith.

I don't think I have ever met a woman as faithful to her husband as Shirley was to me, though I surely didn't deserve it. In our early years I was something of a self-centered jerk and I didn't put Shirley first. Honestly, if I had been her, I would have left me.

In later years I would gain the reputation of being a romantic, but that is the case only because of two things. Shirley was easy to romance, and, I learned in the crucible of life with her to make her, next to God, the center of my world. She always used to joke that she had trained me well, and that if she died before me and I remarried, my wife would owe a tremendous debt to her because she had had to put up with the ignorance of my youth and someone else might reap the benefits in the years to come. Here are some lessons I learned in the forge of Shirley's love and commitment.

People Change

No matter how old they are when two people join together in a relationship, be that marriage or friendship or business or church or any other real relationship, they are going to both change with time. This is especially true of young marriage.

When I first told my parents that I was planning to marry Shirley, they were actually opposed to it. Not, mind you, opposed to Shirley, but to the notion of us getting married so quickly and so young. "Why don't you wait three or four years?" they asked. "You are both going to change so much in the next few years." Of course, we were so lovestruck that we responded with the solid reasoning that, yes indeed, we were in fact going to change a lot in the next few years. So why not get married and change together?

Our first year was the craziest rollercoaster on earth. We loved passionately. We fought like the Hatfields and McCoys. I mean, we fought a lot. Here's the thing, though: as much as we fought, we loved more. A new relationship has growing pains and too many people give up and abandon ship before the boat has had a chance to make it through its first set of rapids.

In the first years of our marriage Shirley followed me from a rent house in Sherman to a rent house in Denison, then to three years of Bible college in San Antonio where she got a job typing railroad claims while I cut hair on the side. We also drove 400 miles round trip every weekend to Zapata where her father was kind enough to take under his wings a 20-year-old know-it-all novice pastor and show him the ropes of ministry.

It was a full five years before the rapids of the river of marriage settled into easy paddling as we both changed tremendously in those formative first years together.

Wherever you may be in your marriage or other relationships, just keep in mind that change is the one constant in life. Your situation will change, your finances will change, your health will change, your understanding will change, your values will change, your theology will change, your tastes will change. That's what the whole "for better or for worse" part of the marriage vows is all about. The one thing that didn't change for us was our commitment to seeking and doing God's will in our lives as best we could.

You will have to make choices in the midst of change, so make sure those choices are made from a God-centered and selfless heart. I am not putting myself forward as an example in this, but I will put Shirley forward. I started out self-centered but she was always a model of putting others first. Husbands, in your marriage put your wife first. In your decisions of where to live and where to work and what to buy and everything else in life, put your wife first. Not that you should be a milquetoast dishrag who just bends to every whim, but in considering all things apply the admonition from Scripture to your own marriage: "Be kindly affectioned one to another in brotherly love, in honor preferring one another." (Romans 12.10)

You are going to change in the years to come. You are going to change together. The question is, will you change for the better?

Worth Fighting For

She said, "Anywhere you're going baby
You just gotta know I'm on your side.
When you climb upon the stallion
You are bound to let him take you for a ride
All the way.

I know I'm still wild enough for you.
You know you, you can always count on me.
Baby we used to be worth fighting for
So tell me, are we?"

-Kris Kristofferson, *Worth Fighting For*

Lesser women would have thrown in the towel, but Shirley was a fighter and she fought for those she loved. She was a she-bear when it came to her children. She was fiercely loyal to her friends, especially when they were down and out or struggling. And she would fight *for* me and sometimes *with* me. Again, I am not putting myself forward as a model of the perfect husband, but I must say here that anything good about me, anything commendable, is the result of Shirley not giving up on me, not letting me go.

One example of my selfish, youthful stupidity: when we were living in Zapata, she was stuck at home with three children under the age of 4, and I was cutting hair through the week in a little shop I'd named Aslan's Lair and working in the church as well. Her brother Jerry owned a video arcade on the edge of town, and I remember one time, before cell phones, when I called her from the shop and said I'd be home around 5:00. Instead, I stopped off at the arcade and sat and played video games with a kid named Mark Davis for over two hours. I showed up at the house sometime between 7:00 and 8:00, and was totally nonplussed that she was upset. Never mind that I had told her I would be there two hours earlier. Never mind that she had been stuck in the house with three babies all day. Never mind that she had cooked supper for me expecting me there around 5. Why on earth was she so upset?

There were a few times when the shoe was on the other foot. For the first few years of marriage, Shirley had a hard time wrestling with the balance of being both her daddy's girl and my wife. Jerry McSorley was a faithful, generous, selfless missionary and pastor who took me under his wing and taught me a lot in my early ministry, but he was also a crusty and sarcastic Irishman who thought his girls were on a pedestal and they thought the same of him (rightly so on both counts). Jerry and I would get crossways with each other over something regarding the church, or regarding theology, or regarding life in general, and Shirley would always side with "Daddy."

Now, the truth of the matter is that more times than not, Jerry was right and I was wrong. But it put a tremendous strain on our early marriage. There were times I would get so frustrated I would walk out the door, get in my car, and just drive through the south Texas desert for hours, fuming and ranting to myself about the feuding with Shirley. But I always came back, and we always worked through it, and we always changed toward the better.

Your relationship isn't going to be perfect. Most likely because of you, not your spouse. But don't walk away from a fight that will shape you into a better man.

Don't throw in the towel. Listen to your wife. Listen to others. Don't be afraid to admit you don't have it all together. Cultivate humility. Scripture tells us, "As iron sharpens iron, so one person sharpens another." (Proverbs 27.17) Being sharpened isn't always easy, and it always involves friction that whets away at our dullness. But we can't be sharp without experiencing the sparks that hone us. And sometimes our wives are the best sharpening blocks we have.

Love Doesn't Have To Be Extravagant

In the early years of our marriage Shirley was the one who did all the bill paying and bookkeeping. I just worked, gave her my money, and didn't think twice about what we had or didn't have. During our first year together I was probably making between $150 and $200 a week, and she was making about the same, not exactly flush with cash as we started carving out our new life together.

Bearing in mind that we were barely making it financially, you may think me foolish for doing extravagant things to show my love. And if that is what you think, you would be completely accurate in your assessment. We could have had a date night at Jack in the Box, and instead I would take Shirley to a nice restaurant that would cost us a whopping $25 for dinner! You laugh, but $25 in 1977 had the same buying power as $103 in 2017. Here we were, barely able to pay bills, and I was going out splurging on steaks. Of course, I wasn't the one having to deal with the mental stress of making ends meet. I laid that burden on Shirley.

Perhaps the dumbest thing I did was in 1978. Remember the brown 1970 Cougar that took me to my first meeting with Shirley? My parents bought that for me when I was a junior in high school, and Shirley had an old Toyota Corolla her parents had gotten for her. One day I decided, without saying a word to Shirley, that I would buy a brand spanking new 1978 Oldsmobile Cutlass Supreme. I have no idea what it cost, but it was completely out of the ballpark of our finances.

I came driving up to our rent house one afternoon hoping to "surprise" Shirley.

And, oh my heavens, was she surprised!
Not, as you might imagine, in a good way.
She couldn't believe I had bought a new
car. She couldn't believe I hadn't discussed
it with her. She couldn't believe that I
thought this would make her happy.
Needless to say, this was a learning
experience for me. We kept the car and
somehow managed to survive but it made
for some extremely tight times.

Sometimes it takes a few whacks to my
head before I learn my lesson, and it took
too many years for me to realize that I
didn't have to be extravagant to show my
love.

Don't live beyond your means. Don't
assume being flashy is being truly
impressive. Extraordinary events, trips,
and gifts should be just that: extraordinary; out of the ordinary; not the
common day-to-day experience of life. It
may be that the best way you can show
your wife how much you love her is by, oh,
I don't know, paying the bills, and doing
the bookkeeping, and taking that load off

her shoulders. Or maybe do the laundry. Or surprise her with a simple picnic and not a new car. "A pretentious, show life is an empty life; a plain and simple life is a full life." (Proverbs 13.7)

People hear "I love you" in different ways. Figure out your wife's love language and don't assume she receives love the same way you do. Maybe your love language is gift giving. Maybe hers is acts of service or words or quality time spent together. Maybe she would appreciate roses, but maybe she would more appreciate you taking out the garbage or doing the dishes. Speak to her in her own language. *Comprende?*

Leaders Follow Too

Shirley and I grew up in a legalistic religious subculture, me more than her. Never mind the subject of drinking alcohol or smoking tobacco - those things weren't even open for discussion among *real*

Christians. I couldn't even go to movies (more about my first movie later).

When I was in elementary school in the little town of Emory, Texas, my mother hung a bra out on the clothesline to dry and some vicious rumor started that she owned a bikini, God forbid! For a while I couldn't drink Coke from a can because someone might see it and think I was drinking a beer (I never figured out why someone would assume the can in the hand of a ten-year-old Pentecostal preacher's son was a beer instead of a Coke). No work could be done on Sunday. A deck of cards was an evil thing. Half the time TV was forbidden in my childhood home. And certainly I couldn't go to high school dances.

Part of that legalism gave me a terror of hell. I remember discussions in my teen years about the theological quandary of a person who lived an upright life but died after committing a sin. "If a person lives a godly life, but smokes a cigarette and then dies before repenting, will he go to hell?"

The "liberals" among us thought God would let that one slide. The more legalistic argued that such a person would split hell wide open. I am not suggesting my parents cultivated all of these particulars in me, but this was the milieu in which I grew up.

My religious culture was also permeated with the idea that the husband was the boss of the marriage, and the wife had to submit in all things except the wicked, sinful, and destructive. Early in our marriage, I thought that I was the husband and that made me the boss, and that made my word the final word. Looking back, I'm amazed that Shirley followed me at all! I was, sometimes, pretty much a jackass; she actually yelled that at me once in a fit of frustrated anger.

It took me many years to come to understand that marriage is a team sport. Husbands and wives work in tandem. There is give and take. There is leaning on one another's strengths and shoring up one another's weaknesses. It was easy for me to quote, "Wives, submit yourselves to your own husbands," but I mostly skipped over the verse before that one: "Submit to one another out of reverence for Christ." (Ephesians 5.21,22)

Sometime in junior high school I discovered *The Tao Te Ching* by Lao Tsu, and I have read it regularly ever since. It is a book of Chinese wisdom written 600 years before Christ was born, and it is fully in keeping with his teachings. Here are my two favorite chapters about leadership:

> *Under heaven nothing is more soft and yielding than water.*
> *Yet for attacking the solid and strong, nothing is better;*
> *It has no equal.*
> *The weak can overcome the strong;*
> *The supple can overcome the stiff.*
> *Under heaven everyone knows this,*
> *Yet no one puts it into practice.*
> *Therefore the sage says:*
>   *He who takes upon himself the humiliation of the people is fit to rule them.*
>   *He who takes upon himself the country's disasters deserves to be king of the universe.*
> *The truth often seems paradoxical.*
> - Chapter 78

Why is the sea king of a hundred streams?
Because it lies below them.
Therefore it is the king of a hundred streams.

If the sage would guide the people, he must
serve with humility.
If he would lead them, he must follow behind.
In this way when the sage rules, the people
will not feel oppressed;
When he stands before them, they will not be
harmed.
The whole world will support him and will not
tire of him.

Because he does not compete,
He does not meet competition.
- Chapter 66

Nowadays that is called "servant leadership." Husbands lead their wives, lead their families, by serving them. I can't encourage you husbands enough to never rely on lording it over your wives. Lead by example. Lead by gentleness. Lead by loving. And, paradoxically, sometimes you lead by following. Jesus taught his disciples to serve others, saying, "For even the Son of Man did not come to be served, but to serve," and, "The greatest among you will be your servant. For those who exalt themselves will be humbled, and those who humble themselves will be exalted." (Mark 10.45, Matthew 23.11-12)

Saint Paul adds, "Have this mind among yourselves, which is yours in Christ Jesus, who, though he was in the form of God, did not count equality with God a thing to be grasped, but emptied himself, taking the form of a servant..." (Philippians 2.5-7)

John Denver's *Follow Me*, which I sang to Shirley at our wedding, has him saying to his beloved, "Follow me, where I go, what I do and who I know." But he ends the song with these words: "Take my hand, and I will follow you."

July 30, 1977. We were married in Denison, TX then
headed off for a cheap honeymoon to Texarkana.

The Swiss Village of Murren. Shirley insisted I take a photo of her "Karate Kid" pose wherever we went.

The renewal of our wedding vows on our 20th anniversary.

Christmas Eve with "K3." Shirley shone in many areas, but maybe she was the brightest and happiest as "Grandma."

Two of our trips: Our 20th Anniversary in Jamaica,
and a writing trip to Merida, Yucatan, Mexico.

"Look at you, still pretty as a picture. Look at me, still crazy over you. Look at us, still believin' in forever. If you want to see how true love should be, then just look at us."

Chapter Four

Two Honeymoons

Did I tell you we didn't have much money when we were first married? The truth of the matter is, we never had much money the rest of our lives, but we did okay and were blessed with many opportunities to travel and experience things around the world. But starting out we had some pretty slim pickings.

Texarkana, Seriously?

When we were planning our wedding, we had absolutely zero money for a honeymoon. Not a nickel. But about four months before the wedding the teacher in my high school government class announced an essay contest being sponsored by the local Chamber of Commerce. The subject was "free enterprise" and there would be awards for high school and college entries. As soon as he said it, I whipped out a pen and paper and wrote an essay during the rest of our class time. As I think back on it now, I realize that was my very first published piece of writing! I submitted the essay and waited. A month later I received notice that I had won first place in the contest, and the award was a check for $300. Shirley and I were overjoyed! We had a whole $300 to spend on our honeymoon!

We did everything on the cheap. Cheap rings (under $150 for both of them), cheap wedding, cheap honeymoon. After the two o'clock Saturday wedding, we changed into our "Just" and "Married" T-shirts, crawled into my uncle's Chevy van (some of you are old enough to remember that era when decked out vans were all the rage), and headed east for our first trip together. As I was driving, Shirley started singing Rod Stewart's *Tonight's The Night*, and I was so inexperienced and embarrassed that I hushed her as if she were citing something deplorable. Somewhere near Paris, Texas we stopped at a little diner and had hamburgers, our first meal as a married couple. Then we made our way to the exciting destination of Texarkana, Texas. To this day I have no idea why we chose Texarkana as our honeymoon destination. I mean, San Antonio would have been just as close; New Orleans not a lot further; even one-hour-away Dallas would have been more exotic!

Our first night together was spent in a Holiday Inn Holidome, and our room, complete with sliding doors that opened out into the dome area, was right next to the shuffleboard court. So we spent our first evening as a married couple listening to the clatter of the shuffleboard and the yelling of children right outside our door. Such romance.

From there we drove - again, I have no idea why - to Idabel, Oklahoma where we ate at a little Italian restaurant and spent the night in a dumpy roadside hotel. But we didn't care because we were in love and just married and nothing else mattered.

We were going to spend two nights in Idabel (again, *why?*) but the room was such a dump that we opted to head back toward home. And that is when we committed our first sin as a married couple. It was August 1, 1977, and *Star Wars* was a hit movie in the theaters. We got a hotel room somewhere in Dallas then made our way to a theater and bought our tickets. We had come to the conclusion that going to G and PG rated movies surely wasn't actually against God's will, but we were as nervous as cats in a room full of rocking chairs as we stood in line for the movie. We kept looking this way and that, praying that no one from church would happen to be around and see us entering such a den of iniquity.

Star Wars was amazing! And the rapture didn't happen while we were inside and us get "left behind." And God didn't strike us with leprosy. And so it was that on our honeymoon I attended the first movie in my life. To borrow a line from one of Shirley's favorite poems, *When I Am An Old Woman*, it was that moment that I began to "make up for the sobriety of my youth."

Three days on the road and we had spent our $300 award money, so we headed back to our little house in Sherman and settled into life together.

Doing It Up Right

During the next 20 years Shirley and I loved to travel. We went places together whenever we could scrape up the money. We took our kids places, figuring that exposure to the wider world was an important point of education. Campouts in the Texas hill country, a vacation to a cabin in Colorado, Disney World in Orlando, a boat ride through the swamps of Louisiana, and of course, trips to "the big cities" nearby, Minneapolis and Saint Paul when we were in Wisconsin, and Dallas and San Antonio when we were in Texas.

But I always felt like I wanted a do-over so I could give Shirley a proper honeymoon. By the time of our 20th anniversary in 1997 I had become a priest and a bishop, and traveled a lot for various church meetings. Sometimes Shirley would get to go along and we would add a day or two to the trips and see the sites nearby. In my traveling with the church, I accumulated a lot of frequent flyer miles and was able to use those as I saw fit.

As you already know, I was something of a romantic klutz and selfish jackass in our early years, and I wanted to make up for that and do something wonderful for Shirley on our first big anniversary. I was such a shy and inexperienced young man that I didn't even propose to Shirley! It just sort of "happened" that we decided to get married. If I remember it correctly, we were sitting in a little restaurant on a cheap date and the topic turned to, "Should we get married? When?" And it just evolved from there.

As our 20th loomed near, I plotted a surprise for my lover who had been so selfless and sacrificial throughout our marriage. I saved money. I connived. I planned in secret. One Sunday morning a month or so before our anniversary, I processed out of church after the service and then paused, took off my vestments, called Shirley out of the congregation, and knelt down on one knee in the middle of the aisle and proposed to her. She said yes (what else could she do?) and the congregation erupted in applause.

After the service our family went out to lunch together and I presented Shirley with a little gift. It was a T-shirt with the symbol of a Jamaican resort on it: for our honeymoon re-do I was taking her to the

Caribbean. I already had the tickets secured and the resort paid for. On the weekend closest to our wedding date my friend Bishop John Holloway from Georgia flew in and celebrated the renewal of our vows. This time Shirley had a beautiful dress and I had a tuxedo. This time I placed a real diamond ring on her finger.

After the ceremony we packed our bags and spent a solid week at an all-inclusive resort in Jamaica. It was the first time in my entire life that I stayed in one place for a whole week: room service any time of the day or night, champagne for the asking, and the biggest decision being, do we go out the front door to the pool or the back door to the beach. We took a lot of trips together over the next 20 years, including going back to the same resort on our 25th anniversary, but in my mind this is still one of the most magical weeks we ever spent together.

Celebrate Your ~~Life~~ Wife

You may be young and not have two nickels to rub together. You may be middle-aged and just struggling to survive. You may have enough money to do anything you want, anytime you want. But I cannot emphasize enough the importance of celebrating your life together with your wife. Plan events or trips and make it a priority to give your wife some quality time and undivided attention.

There is something very important about an occasional change of pace, change of scenery. When we had children at home, Shirley and I made it a practice for just the two of us to get away for a couple of nights at least once a quarter. It didn't have to be extravagant - we would find a cheap hotel room on Priceline and go to Dallas for a short getaway.

For a long time it was our tradition to take a three night post-Easter break in Dallas. Holy Week and Easter were incredibly busy times for us. We had a church service on Maundy Thursday, two on Good Friday, one on Saturday noon, one Saturday night and one Easter morning, followed by a church picnic. At the end of the picnic, we would hop in the car and go spend three nights in the Dallas area just being together. Part of our getaway was a covenant we made with one another that we would not eat in any restaurants we had visited before. This gave us an opportunity to explore new places and new foods, and we discovered some of our favorite restaurants this way.

Some couples, especially those with children, make it a point to go on a date once a week or twice a month. There were times in our lives when Shirley and I would actually make appointments with each other and put it on our calendars. That way, nothing except an emergency was going to keep us from quality time together. "Bishop Ken, can you do thus and so next Friday night?" "Oh, I'm sorry, I already have an engagement that night."

If you don't have children at home, you can have a date night and never leave the house. The key is to be intentional about it. Set aside a time and plan ahead. Cook together. Watch a movie. Go to bed early. Or stay up late and binge-watch a TV series. Or after dinner go for a nice long walk. Or play a board game. You get the idea. But, make it an evening spent with purpose; the purpose, of course, being to build your relationship.

Jesus told his disciples to "come apart into a desert place, and rest a while." (Mark 6.31) I had a Bible college teacher who used to say, "If you do not come apart, you will come apart!" Life has enough wear and tear in it that sometimes we begin to fray, and it is in those "come apart" times that we mend and strengthen the cords of our relationships.

Now, let me share a secret with you that took me too long to learn. In those come-apart times, make the focus about your wife. What does she like to eat? What movie does she want to see? How can she best rest? What would be her idea of a perfect couple of days together? Shape your time with her at the center. And don't forget to throw in a few simple surprises.

One year for her birthday, Shirley wanted to go to Dallas and get Vietnamese food. She had a favorite restaurant and I promised to take her there for dinner. What she didn't know was that all of our kids and grandkids were going to join us as a surprise I had arranged.

The plan was for Shirley and our daughter Stormie and I to arrive at the restaurant, get seated, and about 15 or 20 minutes later the rest of the family would join us. I drove from Denison to Dallas, and when we reached the restaurant it was closed. Crisis mode! What am I going to do? It was ridiculous, trying to communicate via text messaging with the rest of the family, while also trying to find another Vietnamese restaurant, and coordinate the timing of a whole new plan. It started getting preposterous and Shirley, having no idea what game was afoot, started saying, "Just forget Vietnamese. Just find someplace to eat. I'm hungry. I'm tired of driving around." About two minutes later I pulled into the restaurant parking lot and we walked inside to a table full of Myers kids and grandkids all yelling, "Surprise!" She was in heaven, and I was relieved.

You don't have to spend a lot of money or take a long trip. With a little forethought and creativity you can make a single evening spent locally into a memorable time that will restore her soul. Pack some sandwiches and wine, pick your wife up for lunch, and take her on a picnic. Surprise her with breakfast in bed and flowers. Pitch a tent in the back yard and camp out. But don't forget, whether it is a second honeymoon or a special evening at home, make it intentional, and

MAKE IT ABOUT YOUR WIFE.

Chapter
Five

The Rest Of Our Lives

I have written this book for two reasons. First, because so many people asked me to write about the love affair between Shirley and me, and second, because I hope to pass on some hints and ideas to husbands which will perhaps serve as kindling for building the bonfires of their own romance. This book isn't an autobiography; nevertheless, I think it is important to share an overview of our 40 years together.

Follow Me...To Wisconsin

I sang *Follow Me* to Shirley in our wedding, and she did follow me down roads where other women may have balked. She sang, "I'll walk in the rain by your side," and she did walk by my side - in rain, in snow, and into and out of places and churches and religious traditions. In all kinds of conditions and sometimes with great sacrifice, my angel went with me every step of the meandering path of life.

During and after Bible college we spent six years in Shirley's hometown of Zapata, Texas. Her extended family lived on an old military base out in the desert about four miles from town where rattlesnakes, not roses, were more common in the yards. I served in ministry as an assistant to her father, Jerry McSorley, and he taught lessons in life and ministry that I still hold dear to this day. But we also didn't always see eye to eye, and eventually it was time for me to move on.

Leaving Zapata was literally life changing in more ways than one. It was a change of epic proportion because Shirley was leaving her cocoon. She had grown up in Zapata and, other than a couple of years in Sherman/Denison, it had been her home since childhood. She was surrounded by her parents, her sisters, and more nieces and nephews than I could count.

Not long before we left, her father and I came to a disagreement and Shirley found herself for the first time having to decide whether to stand with her dad or her husband. It isn't like Jerry and I were at war with one another, we just came to an impasse on ministry and our future plans. Until now any little disagreements were worked out, and Shirley basically took her father's side because, "He's your boss." But now we had come to a fork in the road, and Jerry was walking down one path and I was walking down the other. Poor Shirley. Neither her father nor I said, "You have to choose," but she was placed in that predicament anyway.

She chose me. And it was hard for her. It changed our relationship immensely. Something happened in her psyche and it somehow hit her that she and I were in this thing called life together, come hell or high water. Until the day she died, Shirley loved her father with all her heart, but she loved her husband in a different and deeper way. Fathers are called to raise their daughters and then release them. Husbands are called to join themselves forever to another man's daughter. The bond is, or should be, deepest between a woman and her husband.

When Shirley had this paradigm shift, our fighting and arguing diminished by an order of magnitude. I mean, I was still a young, inexperienced, self-focused, and occasionally jackassish person, but I was growing up, learning, and becoming my own man. Shirley's love was changing me into a better person.

I prayed and thought and wrestled with the prospects of our future, and I finally talked to Shirley and we agreed that, come

August of 1984, we were leaving her hometown, even if we didn't know where to go. I started praying and looking for other places to serve in ministry and connected with a friend of mine from Bible college. Tim Warner was pastoring in northern Wisconsin and had lunched with a fellow pastor who told him he was resigning. Tim told him about me, and the long story made short is that in the early summer of '84 Shirley and I loaded up our three little children and moved 1,500 miles north to Wisconsin. We spent three glorious years there pastoring some of the best people in the known universe, who took a young 24-year-old pastor and family and loved us, provided for us, and showed us warmth and hospitality beyond measure.

Although it wasn't a place of heat and pressure, Wisconsin served as a kind of forge to bring Shirley and I closer together. We learned to depend on one another more than ever before. Although we were surrounded by love, we still experienced what it meant to be uprooted, moved, and replanted in a different place and culture. Shirley couldn't run across the road to her sister's house; she couldn't walk down the street to Mom and Dad's. I didn't have my father-in-law nearby to give me wisdom or counsel. Life was good, but life was different, and the wonderful years up north made the oneness of our marriage stronger than ever.

Husbands, sometimes life will throw you curve balls. Sometimes plans will change or won't work out at all. Sometimes you may find yourself moving out into uncharted territory. These are not moments to despair or fear, they are opportunities to grow in who you are as a person and who you are as a husband to your wife. Again, the word *intentional* pops up. Use these opportunities with intention. Make them occasions of loving and serving your wife and looking after her needs.

There is an old saying that "The same sun that melts the butter hardens the brick." Any crisis, any change in life, can serve to weaken or strengthen your marriage. What makes the difference is your focus and your intention. Make your wife your focus. Make growing together, even in times of change, your intention.

No Place But Texas

I knew God was calling us to move back to Texas. It was burning in my heart. I loved the people in Wisconsin, but I knew things were about to change. After Shirley and I processed what I was feeling, I told the elders at the church that I felt God was calling us to leave. They told me I was wrong, and asked me to stay one more year. I agreed but the feeling just intensified. I would drive my car out into the beautiful Wisconsin countryside, pop in a cassette of Willie Nelson, and cry like a baby as he sang *No Place But Texas*. It wasn't mere sentimentality or national allegiance - God was pulling at my heart strings.

When I knew that I knew that I knew the time had come to leave, I asked God to let me have a hand in choosing a successor. He brought to mind a pastor I had met at a conference in Atlanta so I called him to check his pulse about the possibility of pastoring in Wisconsin. He wasn't home when I called, but his wife told me, "You're not going to believe this, but Randy is from Wisconsin, and he sat us down last night as a family and said, 'I don't know when, and I don't know how, but God is telling me he's taking us to Wisconsin to pastor!'"

Randy and Ginger Dean came for a visit and I said not a word to the church or leadership about resigning. Randy was just a guest preacher spending a few days with us. The people instantly fell in love with him. One older woman told me after Sunday service, "Pastor Ken, we don't ever want you to leave, but if you ever do, we sure would love to have that young man be our pastor." An elder cornered me later and said, "I don't understand this, but I believe God is saying that Randy is supposed to be here. I don't know, maybe as an assistant pastor or something."

After Randy left, I met with the leadership and said, "I have some good news and some bad news. The bad news is, I know that it is time for me to resign." They all moaned and groaned and said, "Please don't." I said, "And the good news is that Randy Dean is supposed to be your new pastor." To which Alan Wienke, a right-hand man, a stalwart supporter, a dear friend, replied, "So, how soon can you leave?" We all broke out laughing, and we all knew that God was up to something here.

That was 1988. Randy and Ginger have been at Living Word Chapel ever since. We rented a U-Haul, drove it to Texas, unloaded it, traded it off to the Deans, and they loaded it and drove it back. They even bought our house. Smoothest pastoral transition in the history of the world! After I left, Living Word Chapel built an education wing and named it in my honor. To this day I count the Deans and all the folk of that church as some of my dearest friends.

Shirley and the kids and I moved back to Denison, where I had grown up and where we had met. I worked for a short season with my father in his missionary ministry and then was invited to come on staff at Glad Tidings Assemblies of God Church in Sherman. Clyde Causey, the senior pastor, was a man of prayer, depth, and wisdom, and I learned a great deal from him. I served as his associate pastor for two years, then he unexpectedly resigned and I was given the role of senior pastor. That's when everything fell apart - and Shirley followed still.

Crossing the Thames

I discovered church history during my second year at International Bible College in San Antonio. Elwood Jenson was a monotone teacher teaching the boring subject of church history. He also happened to be my favorite teacher on campus. I couldn't wait for his class. I was barbering on the side and I would cut his thick white hair (he always - *always* - said, "make it curly" or "make it red this time," and I always chuckled at his corny jokes) and we would talk history. He took a liking to me and started giving me books out of his 10,000 volume personal library. Other students dropped his class like flies. I hung onto every word he spoke.

One weekend in Zapata, I told my father-in-law about my newfound love for church history. In his typical sarcastic Irish way, he said, "You don't know anything about church history! Here, read this." And he placed in my hands a copy of *The Apostolic Fathers*.

Now, I need to explain something. I was raised Pentecostal (basically Baptist with an added glaze of spiritual gifts), and was under the impression that if St. Paul or one of the other Apostles showed up in town today, they would be most comfortable in our church because it was more like the New Testament church than any other in town. As I picked up *The Apostolic Fathers*, I began reading letters written by men trained and ordained by the Apostles themselves - men who had served under their leadership, followed in their footsteps and died as martyrs for the faith. Men like St. Polycarp of Smyrna, St. Clement of Rome, St. Ignatius of Antioch.

These men were our direct links to the Apostles themselves, and what they were writing was nothing at all like what I was experiencing in church. These men wrote about bishops, which we didn't have. They wrote about liturgy, which we didn't do. They wrote about the Eucharist being the center of worship, whereas we celebrated it whenever the pastor had a whim to do it, maybe three or four times a year. For these men of old, communion was a true reception of the body and blood of Christ; for us communion was a memorial and nothing more.

In the early years of my ministry, my father-in-law and I had a deal: whichever one of us died first, the other one got his library. When Jerry passed away I took only one book from his shelves: that exact copy of *The Apostolic Fathers* that he had loaned me those many decades ago.

This was something of a crisis of faith for me. It set me on a journey that took 12 years to walk out. I began exploring the early church, the Catholic Church, the Orthodox Church, the Anglican Church. I knew that I had to end up in one of these ancient traditions. We moved to Wisconsin, then back to Texas, and worked in non-denominational and Assemblies of God churches, but I knew my journey hadn't ended.

Being associate pastor at Glad Tidings worked well, because I wasn't the one who set the vision of the church; it was my calling to serve Pastor Clyde and the vision he had for the congregation. But when I became senior pastor that all changed. Suddenly I was the vision-caster, and my vision wasn't at all in keeping with the rest of the leadership. We struggled along together for a year or so, but eventually everyone realized this wasn't a marriage made in heaven. I resigned from Glad

Tidings in 1992 and started Christ Church as an intentionally sacramental, liturgical, charismatic, and evangelical congregation. We were alone, but we knew we had to join something older and greater than us.

They call converting to the Catholic Church "crossing the Tiber." They call converting to the Orthodox Church "crossing the Bosphorus." I suppose you might call converting to the Anglican tradition "crossing the Thames." On January 6, 1993, the Feast of Epiphany, I was ordained a priest in God's one, holy, catholic, and apostolic church. Two years later, on June 9, 1995, the Feast of St. Columba, I was consecrated bishop.

For the next 21 years I served as a local pastor and bishop in Sherman. Some days were diamond and some days were stone. I preached, counseled, heard confessions, baptized, married, and buried. Sometimes I saw financial miracles and other times I did without a salary. I ordained deacons and priests and traveled throughout the United States and the world as a bishop. In 2014 I took a terrifying and exciting leap of faith and resigned from pastoral ministry to start Graceworks, a ministry devoted to writing and teaching.

The point of this whole history is to let you know that Shirley was there right beside me, climbing every mountain and pressing through every valley. She celebrated the good times and was a moral and spiritual support in the bad times. She was a discerning radar when I was too thick-headed to see things. She wrestled through converting to the Anglican tradition with great sincerity and with significant opposition from some family members and friends. She didn't just follow me, she owned what we were doing for herself.

We made this spiritual journey together just like we had made physical journeys together in the past. She sang to me the day we married, "I'll walk in the rain by your side, I'll cling to the warmth of your hand, I'll do anything to keep you satisfied, I'll love you more than anybody can." She vowed to stand with me, "for richer or for poorer, for better or for worse." And she did this until the day she died. Let me say it simply: Shirley made me. If Shirley was for me, I could face an army. If she wasn't on the same page, sometimes I felt helpless. I would not be me without Shirley being Shirley right beside me. The only thing I would change if I could go back and do it all over again is that I would listen to her more closely and focus on her more intently.

If you are a husband reading this there is a good chance that I don't know your story or what you are going through right now. I do know that a loving wife makes literally all the difference in how life gets lived out. But this doesn't happen automatically or quickly, neither is it all on your wife's shoulders to be that loving, supporting partner in life.

A lot of the responsibility for making this dynamic happen rests on your shoulders. Clearly God should be at the center of your life. Other than that, there is nothing, and I mean nothing, more important in your daily living than cultivating a solid, loving relationship with your wife. It will cost you. It will inconvenience you. It will also shape and mold you into a better man. And the dividends you reap will be exponential. Put God first. Put your wife second. Put everyone and everything else after that.

Chapter Six

Romancing Your Wife

In this final chapter I hope to share some snapshots of a few romantic experiences I crafted for my sweet Shirley in the hopes that they will give husbands reading this book some springboard ideas for creating their own romantic moments. Don't replicate these (well, one or another may strike your fancy and you can copy it and not even tell anyone it was my idea - I'm nice that way), but use them as starting places for doing your own thing. Just let me drive home the importance of making your wife the center of your attention and your number one priority. Without further ado, here are some celebrations of life that I created for Shirley Mae.

Giving Gifts And Marking Moments

I have already told you about our second honeymoon in Jamaica. Not all of our trips were surprises for Shirley - in fact, only a few were. Most of the time she was involved in travel plans, although she frequently told me to plan it myself because she felt I was pretty good at that sort of thing and she knew she would enjoy whatever we did.

I did have to learn that all travel wasn't about history. I'm a history nut. I could go to England or Italy or Spain and spend the whole time checking out historical sites. Shirley was interested in history too, but she needed to temper that with sightseeing and taking in a theatrical performance or a concert.

She told me once that if it were up to her, we would include some musical experience in every trip we took. To the best of my ability I made that happen for the rest of our travels. Sometimes it was planned with her, sometimes it was a surprise. Sometimes it was a fortuitous circumstance, like discovering that a string quartet was playing Vivaldi's *Four Seasons* in St. Chapelle, perhaps the most beautiful church in Paris.

When I was elected bishop I had the honor of having lunch with the famed Texas jeweler James Avery. We had a wonderful visit together and I told him about my election. I asked him if his company ever made custom pieces like signet rings for bishops and he said that indeed they did. I asked him who to contact about having a ring designed and he said, "Oh, I'm doing this one myself!" He proceeded to pull out a pen and sketch ideas for my seal on a napkin. I still have that napkin to this day! People from our church donated gold to be melted down for the ring and my pectoral cross. To this day, that ring and cross are two of my most prized possessions. They contain the gold of one friend's college class ring, and the gold of one widow's wedding ring.

When James Avery was making my signet ring, which I would use for sealing ordination certificates and other official documents, I had him make a gold pendant of the seal and surprised Shirley with it the night I was consecrated bishop. The first thing I ever set my seal on as a bishop was my dear wife the night I was consecrated.

On her 38th birthday I sought out a local jeweler and took him a .38 special bullet. First I had to remove the bullet from the shell, take out all the powder, then reset the bullet. The jeweler used it to make a wax copy which he then poured silver into. The result was a necklace I placed on her neck, telling her she was my .38 special. She wore it for years and after she passed away I found it in her jewelry box.

Probably the second most magical trip we ever took was on Shirley's 40th birthday. She loved Eric Clapton and had never seen him in concert. So I went to the internet to see if he might be playing anywhere nearby precisely on her birthday. It turns out he was doing a concert in Las Vegas with a full orchestra and Billy Preston on the organ.

I secretly called our dear friends Victor and Debbie Leal and asked if they wanted to join with me and surprise Shirley with a Clapton concert in Vegas. Victor said, "I went to school with a woman who works in management at a hotel in Vegas. Let me call and see if I can get discounted rooms." It turned out that his friend was the group sales manager at the New York, New York casino and hotel, and she comped us two suites and dinner at the hotel. Each suite was a high-floor corner room with an in-room Jacuzzi.

When we went down for dinner the hostess looked at the card Victor handed her and had a surprised look on her face.

Victor asked her why the surprise and she said, "This is a full comp! It doesn't happen very often. This means everything is on the house: cocktails, appetizers, dinner, dessert, wine, everything." We had an amazing meal with great wine. When it came time for dessert, the waitress brought over a tray showing us all our options. As we dilly-dallied around trying to figure out which magnificent desserts we should choose, she said, "Oh, it's all on the house, I'll just bring you one of everything" So there we sat before heading to the concert, nibbling on about eight different decadent desserts!

Clapton was at his best, and Billy Preston played without doubt the best piece of organ music that rock music has ever produced (go to YouTube and check out the video *Have You Ever Loved A Woman?* from the *One More Car; One More Rider* tour). Shirley was in her element and loved every minute of it. After the show we walked back to the hotel and as we were headed to the room Victor said, "Y'all go on up, I'm going to play a little poker before I go to bed." The next morning he informed us that he had won enough to pay for our plane and concert tickets. In other words, I planned this special celebration for my angel, and the whole thing ended up being completely free!

For one birthday, I can't remember which or why, I did a "Queen of Hearts" theme for Shirley. I found a cool Queen of Hearts T-shirt for her based on Alice in Wonderland (a play she loved and had acted in as a girl). I searched the internet for ideas and ran across a tiny ceramic case in the shape of three stacked cards that was just big enough to hold a piece of jewelry. I then found a nice little silver pendant of a Queen of Hearts which I placed into the case. Finally, I took a new deck of cards, cut the center out of the middle forty or so cards, glued them all together, and made a top and bottom out of the rest of the cards. I placed the little case with the pendant inside the cards then put them back into the box. Her gift that year was a box of cards. Her surprise was what was inside.

Shirley was born in 1958 so when she turned 50 I found a Ben Franklin silver half dollar from the year she was born and had it mounted as a pendant.

Every year of marriage has a substance it is associated with - silver for the 25th, gold for the 50th. Well, it turns out the 30th anniversary is pearl. I didn't have a lot of money on hand to celebrate our 30th, but I thought ahead and saved up some money and did what I could. First, I bought Shirley a Janis Joplin T-shirt (Janis' nickname was Pearl). I also got her a copy of John Steinbeck's *The Pearl*. Oh, and I got her a moderately priced pearl necklace with matching earrings. I found a place online that made custom wrapping paper. You just load up an image and they do the rest. So I wrapped all her gifts in paper that was covered with images of Vermeer's painting, *Girl With A Pearl Earring*.

The icing on the cake was our overnight trip to Dallas. We stayed at a nice hotel on Pearl Street, and went to hear some music

at a little place called Blues on Pearl. Right
about now you are probably saying to
yourself, "Well, *that* was a little over the
top," and it probably was. But it was fun to
plan it, and Shirley loved it, and it made a
memory she kept with her the rest of her
life.

The Sound Of Music

I have written 10 books and half of
them were written in the Mexican city of
Merida, Yucatan. My method is to study
and research the subject, and maybe even
teach on it for a while, making it mine
before I set it down on paper. But when it
comes time to actually write, I get away to
some secluded spot and from the time I
wake up until the time I go to bed I write,
taking a short break for lunch and dinner.
My favorite place to write is on the little
patio attached to my hotel room in the
courtyard of the Luz En Yucatan hotel. It
is a small 17-room hotel that was a former
18th century convent.

Shirley went with me each time I wrote a book, and while I was steadily typing away she would relax, read a book, soak in the pool, or go for a walk in the city. I would take a break for lunch, or sometimes she would go across the street to a little cafe and bring lunch back to the room. In the evenings we would find a great restaurant in town (Merida is full of great restaurants) and Shirley and I would leisurely enjoy dinner together, and maybe even hire a horse and buggy for an hour-long ride through the city. After dinner it was back to the keyboard for me while Shirley unwound and went to bed without me. I would come crawling into bed beside her when I was too tired to write more.

The next book on my agenda was going to be titled *How Christians Pray*, a detailed study of the Lord's Prayer. As was my custom, I had done all the study for it, researched every resource I could find, taught it for 12 weeks in a class, and now the only thing left was to get away and actually write it. One day we were watching TV and a commercial came on that had snow falling in the background. Shirley said, "I miss the snow so much," so I suggested that for the next book we go somewhere with snow. She responded, "No, because that time is about you, not me. You need to write where you are most comfortable, and you couldn't sit outside and write where it was snowy - we should just go back to Merida." I told her to leave it to me and I would figure something out.

That's when I started lying to her. I told her I had found a place in upstate New York that was somewhat rustic but in a beautiful setting, and although we were going in August and there wouldn't be snow, there would still be cool temperatures and we could enjoy brisk walks through the hills when I took a break from writing. I told her to pack warm clothes and shoes she could hike in. Then, I set myself on a secret mission to actually write the book and get it published before we went on the trip.

Shirley's birthday is August 13, and our schedule called for us to be on this "writing trip" (but remember, I had already written the book) that same week. We boarded the plane in Dallas and headed toward New York City. I happened to have enough bonus points with the airline at the time to upgrade us to first class, and after we took off I said to Shirley, "I know it isn't your birthday until tomorrow, but I'm going to be busy writing, so I want to give you your little gifts early."

I asked the flight attendant to bring us champagne, and then I gave her the first gift. It was a proof copy of *How Christians Pray*, and the book was dedicated to her. When she unwrapped it she had a puzzled look on her face and I said, "The point being, I'm not getting away to write. That's already done. I'm getting away to spend time with you." Of course, she cried and hugged me and was thrilled that we were having a non-working vacation together.

She unwrapped the second gift, put two and two together, and started sobbing. It was a piece of Swiss chocolate in the shape of a Swiss army knife. The final touch was handing her another airplane ticket, from New York to Zurich. I said, "Baby, we're not going to New York, we're going to spend ten days in Switzerland."

When Shirley was a little girl she loved the movie *The Sound of Music*, and had fantasized since childhood about going to Switzerland. Now her dream was coming true. We landed in Zurich then caught a train that took us through the beautiful Swiss countryside to the valley town of Lauterbrunnen from which we took a cog train 1500 feet up the side of a cliff into the village of Murren. This small piece of paradise is a pedestrian-only village set on the edge of a cliff surrounded on all sides with spectacular vistas of the Swiss Alps.

We spent five days in Murren hiking along mountain trails, taking a cable car to the peak of Schiltorn, and meandering through the Lauterbrunnen Valley, which I found out later was the inspiration for Tolkien's elvish city of Rivendell. We ate delicious food, including one dinner of horse steak which we both had to try because we had never eaten horse before. Someone later asked me what horse steak tastes like and I replied, "A lot like beef, only horsier."

From there we spent a few nights in Lucerne where we walked around the city and went on a cruise across Lake Lucerne. Then we spent a final night in Zurich exploring the beauty of that city.

The entire trip was all about Shirley. It was the crown jewel of my surprises for her throughout our life together. And I pulled it off without a single problem. Later, when women heard about it, they told me that was the most romantic thing they'd ever heard of. One husband jokingly said, "Great. Now you've set the bar too high. The rest of us will never be able to top that one!" It was a once-in-a-lifetime trip to the most beautiful place I had ever seen with the most beautiful woman I had ever known. It was my opportunity to spoil her completely.

I realize that not every husband reading this book can do something this extravagant. Truth be known, I couldn't do it again. It truly was a once in a lifetime thing, but Shirley was worth every bit of planning and every penny I had to save to make it happen.

If you are a husband reading this book, don't feel like you have to do something this grand, but you can do grand things on a smaller scale. There is more love and meaning in the very fact that you would devote time and planning and resources than in the destination you choose.

The point is, love your wife. Serve your wife. Do things for her and not just for yourself. Listen to her. Know what she loves. Know what turns her on. Know what makes her heart skip a beat and puts a twinkle in her eyes. Know her dreams and wishes. Know what makes her tick.

Love The Fire Out Of Your Wife

The day Shirley passed away I received a message from a young man who had been married only a short while. He wrote to tell me that he had kept up with Shirley and me for a while, had read my updates while she was in the hospital, and had grieved when he read of her death. He told me that he was praying for me and that the romance he had seen between Shirley and me served as an inspiration for him and his wife.

I responded to his note with these words:

Thank you for your kind words. Treasure her, my friend. Treasure every day. Every conversation. Every moment of laughter. Man, even treasure your arguments and disagreements. I'd give the moon to get into a tiff with my wife right now. God bless you and your future. We were both 18 when we got married, and this July we were going to celebrate our 40th anniversary. Our love for one another grew - it increased as the years rolled by. I never loved her more than I did today.

If you are a husband reading this book, you can forget everything else I have written but take this to heart: love your wife. Love her like crazy. Love the fire out of your wife. That's all there is to it.

Postscript

I trust that in some small way this little book of stories: beginnings and endings, joy and grief, romance and tiffs, will be of help to other people, especially other husbands. C.S. Lewis has helped tens of thousands with his book *A Grief Observed*, written just a couple of months after his wife, Joy Davidman, passed away. I have written this from the little home pub of my dear friends Deacon Mathew and Kristina Allen in Phoenix, Arizona, seven months after losing my Shirley.

I have no idea what my future holds. Experiencing the untimely death of someone dear to you has a way of clarifying that we are mortal and we don't get to choose our day of departure. I could live another 25 years. I could die before I wake up tomorrow. I have no idea if I will remain single the rest of my life or if I will find a wonderful woman with whom to share my years. The future is unwritten and unseen. After losing Shirley I am learning to cherish every day more than I used to; every conversation with a friend, every beautiful sunset, every word of love from my children, every embrace from my grandkids. Life is precious. I'm going to live it with intention and with attention.

What I do know is I will never lose my sense of romance, for I believe that life itself is romance. God created this world out of love, and he joined himself to it in Christ and redeemed it out of that same love. Love is what makes the world go around. And true love is chock full of romance. The day I stop being romantic is the day I stop living, and I intend to live forever in the new creation, so I expect I'll be romantic then and there too.

What I do know is I am going to continue celebrating acts of romance with other people. I'm going to keep planning surprises for those I love. I'm going to keep giving gifts to friends I cherish. I'm going to live my life intentionally and with as much beauty as I can muster.

And what I do know is, no matter where my life takes me, there'll never be another person quite like Shirley Mae McSorley Myers.

Acknowledgements

This book was born as the result of the ongoing encouragement of several of my friends, especially Catherine Partain who was the first to encourage me to write it. A special thank you to Susan Lipka, Jennifer Paul, Bryan Peach, Fr. David Zampino, and Jane Zavala for their wise editorial suggestions.

About the Author

Kenneth Myers was born in 1959 in Denison, Texas. The son of a pastor/missionary, he married Shirley McSorley in 1977. They have three children and five grandchildren. He is an Anglican bishop and director of Graceworks Teaching Ministry.

www.kennethmyers.net

Made in the USA
Columbia, SC
20 July 2021